📖 READERS

Pre-level 1

Fishy Tales
Colorful Days
Garden Friends
Party Fun
In the Park
Farm Animals
Petting Zoo
Let's Make Music
Meet the Dinosaurs

Duck Pond Dip
My Dress-up Box
On the Move
Snakes Slither and Hiss
Family Vacation
Ponies and Horses
Cuentos de Peces *en español*
Dias Ilenos de color *en español*

Level 1

A Day at Greenhill Farm
Truck Trouble
Tale of a Tadpole
Surprise Puppy!
Duckling Days
A Day at Seagull Beach
Whatever the Weather
Busy Buzzy Bee
Big Machines
Wild Baby Animals
A Bed for the Winter
Born to be a Butterfly
Dinosaur's Day
Feeding Time
Diving Dolphin
Rockets and Spaceships
My Cat's Secret
First Day at Gymnastics
A Trip to the Zoo
I Can Swim!
A Trip to the Library
A Trip to the Doctor
A Trip to the Dentist
I Want To Be A Ballerina
Animal Hide and Seek

Submarines and Submersibles
Animals at Home
Let's Play Soccer
Homes Around the World
LEGO: Trouble at the Bridge
LEGO: Secret at Dolphin Bay
Star Wars: What is a Wookiee?
Star Wars: Ready, Set, Podrace!
Star Wars: Luke Skywalker's
    Amazing Story
Star Wars Clone Wars: Watch Out
    for Jabba the Hutt!
Power Rangers Jungle Fury: We are
    the Power Rangers
A Day in the Life of a Builder
A Day in the Life of a Dancer
A Day in the Life of a Firefighter
A Day in the Life of a Teacher
A Day in the Life of a Musician
A Day in the Life of a Doctor
A Day in the Life of a Police Officer
A Day in the Life of a TV Reporter
Gigantes de Hierro *en español*
Crías del mundo animal *en español*

A Note to Parents

DK READERS is a compelling program for beginning readers, designed in conjunction with leading literacy experts, including Dr. Linda Gambrell, Distinguished Professor of Education at Clemson University. Dr. Gambrell has served as President of the National Reading Conference, the College Reading Association, and the International Reading Association.

Beautiful illustrations and superb full-color photographs combine with engaging, easy-to-read stories to offer a fresh approach to each subject in the series. Each DK READER is guaranteed to capture a child's interest while developing his or her reading skills, general knowledge, and love of reading.

The five levels of DK READERS are aimed at different reading abilities, enabling you to choose the books that are exactly right for your child:

Pre-level 1: Learning to read
Level 1: Beginning to read
Level 2: Beginning to read alone
Level 3: Reading alone
Level 4: Proficient readers

The "normal" age at which a child begins to read can be anywhere from three to eight years old. Adult participation through the lower levels is very helpful for providing encouragement, discussing storylines, and sounding out unfamiliar words.

No matter which level you select, you can be sure that you are helping your child learn to read, then read to learn!

LONDON, NEW YORK, MUNICH,
MELBOURNE, AND DELHI

Written by Fiona Lock

Series Editor Deborah Lock
U.S. Editor John Searcy
Project Art Editor Mary Sandberg
Production Editor Siu Yin Chan
Production Claire Pearson
Jacket Designer Mary Sandberg

Reading Consultant
Linda Gambrell, Ph.D.

First American Edition, 2009
09 10 11 12 13 10 9 8 7 6 5 4 3 2 1
Published in the United States by DK Publishing
375 Hudson Street, New York, New York 10014

DK books are available at special discounts when purchased in bulk for sales
promotions, premiums, fund-raising, or educational use.
For details, contact:
DK Publishing Special Markets
375 Hudson Street
New York, New York 10014
SpecialSales@dk.com

A catalog record for this book
is available from the Library of Congress
ISBN: 978-0-7566-4295-2 (Paperback)
ISBN: 978-0-7566-4294-5 (Hardcover)

Color reproduction by Colourscan, Singapore
Printed and bound in China by L Rex Printing Co., Ltd.

The publisher would like to thank Elizabeth Bartlett
as equestrian consultant.
The publisher would also like to thank the following for their kind
permission to reproduce their photographs:
a=above; b=below; c=center; l=left; r=right; t=top
Alamy Images: Tim Graham 20-21; Peter Llewellyn 17c; Lourens
Smak 15tr. **Corbis:** Walter Bieri / EPA 22t; Christopher Cormack 27t;
Ariel Skelley 7t. **DK Images:** Mr. and Mrs. Dimmock 8br, 9bc; John
Goddard Fenwick and Lyn Moran 22bl; Haras National de Compiegne,
France 19bc; Miss. H Houlden 7bl, 7fbr; Stephen Oliver 6c, 16br, 17bc,
21br, 21fbl; Stephen Oliver / Courtesy of Sally Chaplin 29br, 29fbl;
Darwin Olsen, Kentucky Horse Park, USA 8bl, 9bl, 9fbr; Pegasus
Stables, Newmarket 24br, 25bl. **FLPA:** Gerard Lacz 18-19, 30bl. **Getty
Images:** Gallo Images / Travel Ink 4-5. **Masterfile:** R. Ian Lloyd 28-29.
Photolibrary: Creatas 12-13. **Shutterstock:** Condor 36 31br; Dennis
Donohue 24-25; Kondrashov MIkhail Evgenevich 16t. **Still Pictures:**
Biosphoto / Klein J.-L. & Hubert M.-L. 14-15. **SuperStock:**
Age Fotostock 30-31.
Jacket images *Front:* **Getty Images:** National Geographic /
Ralph Lee Hopkins.
All other images © Dorling Kindersley
For further information see: www.dkimages.com

Discover more at

www.dk.com

Contents

READERS

LEARNING
pre-level
1
TO READ

Ponies and Horses

DK Publishing

Welcome to
the stable yard.
The horses are
eating and drinking.

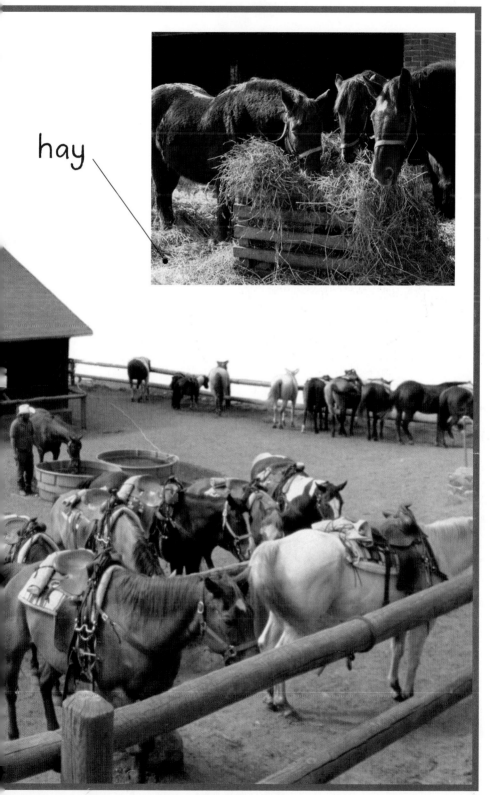

hay

The pony has to be brushed and washed.

brush

grooming kit

brown horses

The brown horse
has horseshoes
fitted to its hooves.

horseshoe

The rider puts a saddle on the palomino [pal-uh-MEE-no] pony.

saddle

 palomino ponies

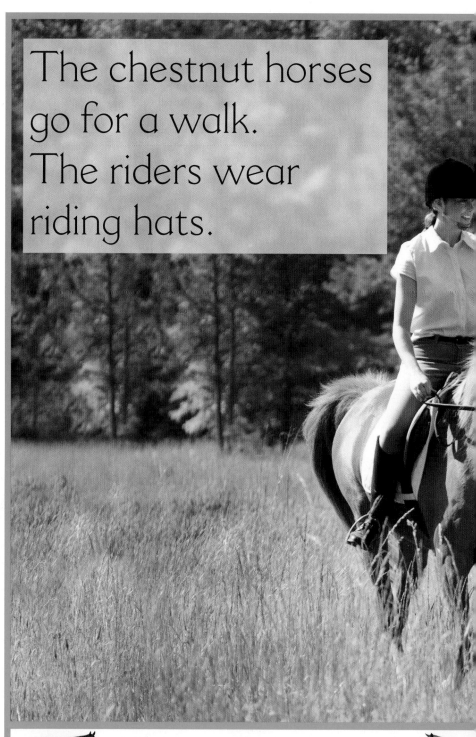

The chestnut horses go for a walk. The riders wear riding hats.

 chestnut horses

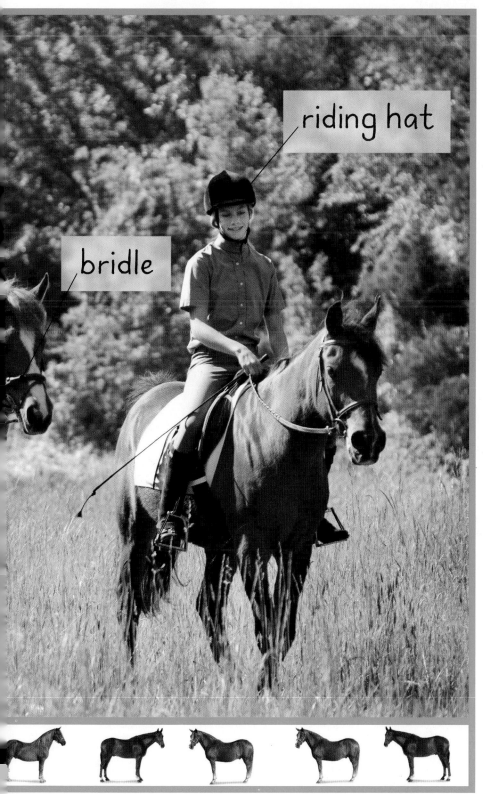

riding hat

bridle

The horse and its foal graze in the field.

foals

foal

black horses

People watch
the black horses at
the horse show.

stirrup

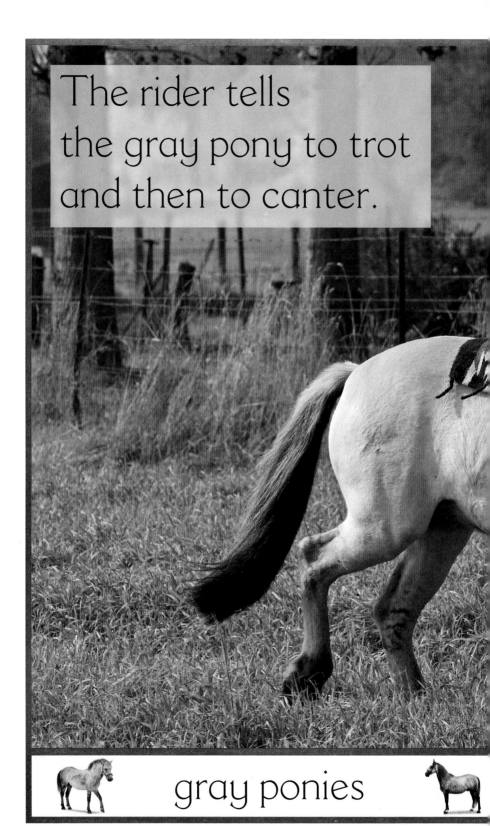

The rider tells
the gray pony to trot
and then to canter.

gray ponies

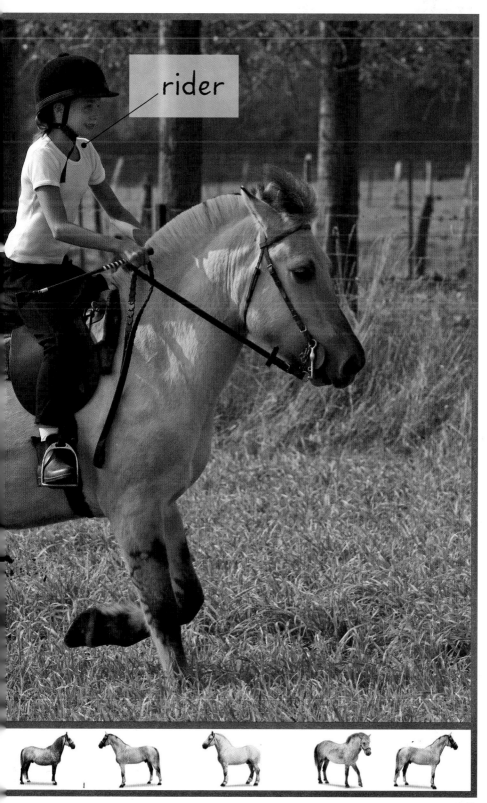

rider

The bay horse jumps over the fence.

fence

 bay horses

dancing horses

The dancing horses jump and leap.

hoof

jockey

racehorses

The racehorses race around the track. Who will win?

track

polo stick

polo ponies

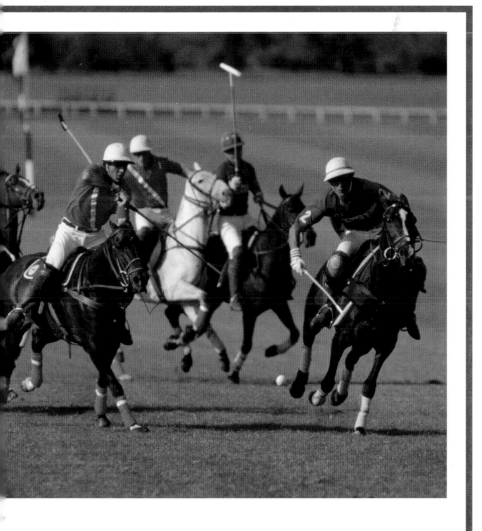

The polo ponies
run up and down
the polo field.

Cowboys ride
ranch horses to
round up the cattle.

 ranch horses

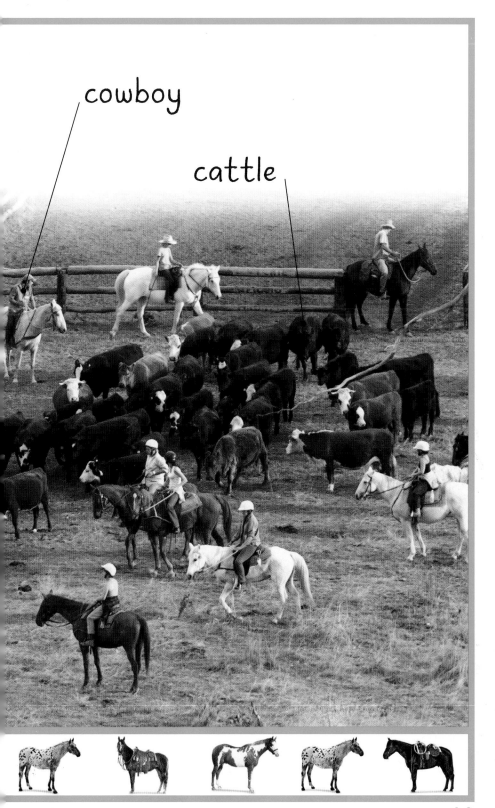

cowboy

cattle

The wild horses gallop across a river.

 Can you gallop

like a horse?

Glossary

 Brush a tool for brushing the hair of a horse

 Fence a row of bars for a horse to jump over

 Hooves the feet of a horse

 Riding hat a hard hat that a horse rider wears

 Saddle a seat for a rider that is tied onto a horse's back

Index